How to ^ *Potty* Train Your ~~Dragon~~ Child

Stephanie Berk, Ph.D.

Preface

There are many books, videos, and products you can buy online now to "help" you potty-train your child. These methods promise success in time frames ranging from 3 days to 3 months. As a mother of 4 boys, with a degree in Human Development and Family Studies from Cornell University, and a Ph.D. in Experimental Psychology from University of Connecticut, I feel comfortable in saying that there is a method that will work for everyone, but not one particular method that will work for every child.

With this in mind, I have written a short booklet that details one method that has worked for my four boys (and 3 other children so far, whose parents have tried it). It should be clear, that like "quick weight loss" programs that promise results to one and all, a certain amount of skepticism is prudent, especially when larger sums of money are involved. I am not promising results guaranteed, but for as much as a gourmet cup of coffee, you will have a 6 chapter booklet, written in easy to understand, concise language, that will aid you in the potty-training of your child. If it works, great- you are done with diapers. If it doesn't work for your family, you have lost little financially, but have gained insight.

You may be wondering why I took the time to write this booklet, and why the price is so low. Quite simply, I enjoy writing, I believe that a booklet should be affordable, and one of my children's teachers suggested I write it, since she had never seen a child potty-train as happily and quickly as mine did. I feel that potty-training can be stressful for parents and for children, so if my experience and knowledge can assist any family in making the transition from diapers to underwear easier, I am more than happy to have helped.

CONTENTS

ACKNOWLEDGMENTS

Even short booklets like this one are never done well, without support. I would like to thank, and acknowledge the support and help from my husband, Mish, my sister Lauren, my friends and colleagues Lori, Becca, Liz, and Leslie, and our babysitters Blair and Erica. I would also like to thank my four boys, Sam, Ben, Matthew, and Gabriel for improving upon my textbook education of child development. I hope all of the readers of this booklet find it to be a resource with implications not just for potty-training, but for other parent-child interactions as well.

How to ^ *Potty* Train Your ~~Dragon~~ Child

1 POTTY-TRAINING

I.a. What is potty-training?

This is a question that most people believe they know the answer to, until they think about, or actually begin to "potty-train" their own child, that is. All of a sudden it becomes an overwhelming, under-informed task, in part because of the sea of conflicting information and advice that is out there, and in part because the vocabulary is not standardized. Not only is there no "how to" manual that works for everyone, but even the definition of "potty-training" is different. Some of these differences are based on both biological and cultural expectations.

With our firstborn, we had many people, ranging from well-meaning older family members to the mailman tell us when and how to potty-train our child. Some people told me that young, American parents are just lazy, and wait too long. Others told me that I would be crazy to try to potty-train my child before he was 3 years old, since the range was 2-4 years; later for boys. One person told me that I should wait until summer time, when I could just let him run around outside naked. Someone else told me to wait until winter when it was too cold and dark for him to want to be outside.

Honestly, I learned to nod my head politely, and thank everyone for their suggestions. Then I looked at my child, hit the academic research studies, and worked out what was best for my child and my family. Here is what I learned that I found helpful. First the definition of "potty-training" differs based on what resources you have available to you, like diapers, ability to discard or wash diapers, time to stay home and attend singularly to your child, and what you mean by potty-training, e.g. sphincter control and urge awareness versus regularity and a schedule.

In communities where the diapers are not as effective as plastic diapers, and/or it is hard to wash and clean the soiled diapers, there is more motivation for finding the quickest way into underwear. In countries, such as the former Soviet Union, and China, among others, children are said to be "potty-trained" as young as 6 months. In these countries and cultures, there is almost always an adult family member with the child for the first one to two years. In China there are special pants that are crotchless, to make it easier to not "wet one's underwear". This "elimination communication" method of potty-training utilizes more of a classical conditioning style that relies more on the adult's recognizing and regularizing a child's schedule, and less on when the child is able to recognize that he/she has an urge to void. While this works for some families and children, it does not work for all, hence I will not focus on this method in the rest of this booklet.

In communities where the diapers are effective, the parents work outside the house, or it is easier to use the diapers for a longer period of time, the pressure to potty-train early is relaxed. This allows for the ability to potty-train at a later age, when the child is aware of his/her own needs, and can even voice them. At this point, the child is able to learn to "hold it" until a potty can be found. At this point, the child can recognize the difference between whether he/she has to "pee" or "poop". And at this point the child can tell the present adult that he/she has to use the bathroom.

There are two sets of 3 phrases that are tremendously important to the success of your child becoming potty-trained; namely the "3Cs" and the "3Pros". The "3Cs" refer to Communication, Consistency, and Commending. The "3Pros" refer to the Process, the Progress, and the Problems. Some of the most important aspects of potty-training 18-48 month olds is communication, and a consistency, by the parents of both effort and vocabulary. You need to decide which words to use. We use "pee pee" and "poopie" or "poop". We call the toilet "a potty". It really doesn't matter which words you use, so long as you are consistent and use them frequently with the children, so that they can learn the words too. (Appendix 1 has a list of potty words, both common and less so. I am sure that there are others that are not listed here.)

Another really important element is commending the child OFTEN! What is such an easy thing for us as adults to do, is really still quite difficult for the young child. We must remember to praise and verbally reward him/her throughout the Process. The goal is to encourage self- motivation and pride.

1.b. Why potty- train now?

You have bought this booklet, so you are obviously thinking of potty-training your child. For some of you, you have decided to read a little early to see how to prepare for this next accomplishment. For others, you are trying to potty-train now and are looking for tips. Still others may have tried everything else, and are thinking that this is your last resort. It doesn't matter why you picked up this booklet, the point remains that you think that your child should be potty-trained, most likely soon.

Fortunately, or unfortunately, potty-training cannot always be when the parent wants it to occur. There are definitely some clues that need to be both evaluated and assessed. Most people get the following advice: 1) If my child expresses an interest, I should potty-train him/her immediately and it will happen quickly. 2) Once the child is potty-trained it will be easier for the parents/ caregivers. 3) If everyone else in your playgroup is potty-training, it is a good time for you to do it too.

All of these pieces of advice have elements of accuracy. For example, if your child does not express an interest or fights you, you should wait a bit and try again in a different way. You don't want to force your child if he/she isn't ready, or if he/she turns it into a control

3

battle. If your child does express an interest, that is great. You can test out how much your child comprehends. Even with an interest, potty-training won't happen automatically. The first sign of interest could be a passing phase. Waiting a few more months will not make a huge difference, if you are verbally encouraging your child.

So what about it being easier to have the child potty-trained? Take a moment to think about what that actually means. When a child is potty-training or even newly potty-trained, travel is very difficult- be it to the store or on a vacation. Going to restaurants is also tedious. You must rely on public bathrooms, and the ability to stop whatever you are doing and where, to be able to go and use the bathroom when the child says so. It is not uncommon for one, potty-training child to use the potty numerous times in succession, at a new place. If there are young siblings, everyone must go to the bathroom. At restaurants, going to the bathroom about 6 times during one meal is comically challenging. It often leads to food and drinks being cleared prematurely, or worse having the server think you bailed on the bill.

Even when a child seems to be doing great with using the bathroom, it is not uncommon for "new events", to throw the child off and accidents will happen. This mess is definitely not easier than diapers. It does not make sense to potty-train your child if you will be traveling soon after. It does not make sense to potty-train your child if he/she is not feeling well, e.g. sick or over-tired. It does not make sense to potty-train your child if you don't have the time for Consistency. "Using the potty" is not easier until your child has passed the "new potty user" phase.

Okay then, what about the argument of: If everyone in the playgroup is potty-training, it is also good for your child? This advice is trickier to assess. On the one hand, if your child potty-trains at the same time, you (the adult) have other people to discuss the 3 "Pro-'s" with: the Process, the Progress, and the Problems. On the other hand, peer pressure is hardly ever a good reason to start doing something. Neither is it really a good method for encouraging self-motivation, consistency, and pride. (If you think back to your days in elementary school, when they taught about peer pressure, it rarely resulted in good outcomes, right?)

One of the Problems of potty-training in groups is that there is the possibility that the child him/herself will decide to be different from everyone else. He/She can turn it into a battle of control, or wills. When this occurs, the adult is more likely to bond with the other adults against the child, and one-on-one Communication with the child about the issue of potty- training decreases. This does not often lead to an easy or good outcome with potty-training for the child.

So, why potty-train now? The reason to potty-train should be based on when the child is ready to use the potty AND when the adult(s) has/have the time and energy to devote a solid 2 weeks to the Process. I am not trying to scare anyone away, but it is kind of like buying a new pet. It does not work well to buy the new pet and then figure out how to take care of it and how much time to spend with it. Often, the pet gets returned to the pet store. In the case of potty-training, the fewer false starts you have, the better everyone ends up being, and the more positive the experience will be.

1.c. Is it harder to potty-train a boy?

As a researcher, this is a really tough question because this should be an empirical question, answered with DATA. I have done an extensive literature search, 4 separate times over the past 9 years. Each time I have met frustration face to face. There are a number of case studies with "atypical" children. There are several studies of potty-training children with developmental differences, including autism-spectrum, and Down's Syndrome. Many of the studies were conducted in the early 1970s, and none of them specifically address the issues that most parents want to know more about. There are MANY "how-to" guides a parent can read online, from diaper companies, Dr. Sears/ Dr. Brazelton, pediatric and or other pediatric/ medical sites. And there are a few articles that look at potty-training cross- culturally and across socio-ethnic groups. (I have many of these in the References section, so that you can find and read them if you are interested.)

5

None of the studies I have found show clear evidence that it is easier to potty-train a girl. None of them find that it is easier to potty-train a boy. Therefore, I am going to refer back to the "3Cs" and "3Pros" that I wrote about earlier: Communication, Consistency, and Commending are essential to the Process, Progress, and even Problems of potty- training, regardless of gender. Until I see a solid research study controlling for method of potty-training, similarity of participants, and time period studied, I must go on with the hypothesis that boys and girls can be potty-trained at the same potential age/level of readiness. (I am not saying that gender differences don't exist. They do. However, with potty-training, I feel that each child should be assessed as an individual, not as a gender, in regards to readiness.)

For the rest of this booklet, I am going to discuss important aspects of what to consider for beginning the potty-training of your child, including timing, materials needed, a schedule, and some problems you might encounter. My hope is that you will be able to take away from this an idea of what might work best for your family, and also that while a bit tedious, potty-training can be a wonderful bonding experience for you with your child. Most people hear the phrase, "Don't worry, it will happen sooner or later. Very few people walk down the aisle, or even go to kindergarten for that matter, in diapers."

That phrase rarely worked for me. I, personally, found it to be negative. Potty-training doesn't have to be an ordeal. It can be a time to read more books, talk more, and spend more time with your young child.

(Free images, 2012)

2 WHEN TO BEGIN POTTY-TRAINING?

2.a. Language knowledge

If you are waiting for your child to show you signs of "potty-training readiness", often they will be language related ones, either spoken or signed. Two of the "3Cs" directly need language specifically. It is hard to have Communication and Commendation without language. Two of the aspects of language that need to be considered are production and comprehension. Production refers to what the child actually says, while comprehension refers to what the child understands. A child might not yet speak in full, clear sentences, e.g. "wan ilk" for "I want milk". However that same child may go and retrieve a blue ball when asked to go get said ball from a pile of multi-colored ones. Hence the comprehension of language is considered better than the production.

It would not be surprising to you if a researcher told you that children comprehend language before they produce it. It would not be a surprise to researchers if you, as the parent, responded with a sarcastic, "Ya think?" Often parents feel disconnected from both researchers and doctors. Language use and potty-training do not need to fall into this "disconnect". Instead a "team approach" should be encouraged, with everyone recognizing that potty-training is a Commitment of both time and language.

This is important because if you are going to rely on the use of language to assist you with the process of potty-training, you must think about what your particular child can understand and say. If you think that your 19 month old can easily say and understand "defecate" and "urinate", you may use those words. If you think that there might be words that are easier and more fun for you and your child to be using over and over again in the next few months, you probably want to choose those. If you suspect that your child has a global language delay, you may want to think about waiting to potty-train your child. If he/she seems to understand everything, but not be very talkative, you may want to give it a shot. Obviously, if you have concerns, you should discuss them with your child's pediatrician. The goal is to use language as a strategy for success, as opposed to a fall into frustration.

The potty-training schedule I have used, and write about in an upcoming chapter, uses language first as a way of both seeing how ready a child is to potty- train, and then as a way to prepare him/her for the big change that is about to occur. It also uses language as a reward and reinforcement of an attempted job well done. There are many wonderful things you can say to your child to reward and reinforce using the potty. You can find several of them in Appendix 2. This is provided because often, we get tired of hearing ourselves saying the same things over and over again. The children probably feel the same way. It is nice to be able to change it up occasionally.

When to start potty-training your child, using the schedule I use, depends on the child having enough language comprehension and then production to be able to be an active partner in the potty-training process. For my own 4 children based on language knowledge, the age range of beginning to potty-train was from 16 months to 30 months, depending on which child it was.

2.b. *Timing issues*

Timing is key to the success of a potty- training attempt. You need to find an interval of time where you can follow the schedule, including "talk" time. It is crucial that communication starts earlier than the actual potty- training attempt and that it continues throughout. For some children, it can be a short lead up as I have in the schedule. For others, you may want weeks, (or months for older children), of letting the child know that there will be a change occurring. This really depends on the personalities of the children and adults who are involved.

When I think my child is getting close to starting the potty-training process, I buy a smaller size pack of diapers. I time the diaper package to finish at about the same time as the potty-training attempt begins. I am able to show the child how the diapers are disappearing. I can tell the child that I will be home for 2 weeks soon, and we will have a great time learning how to use the potty. I discuss how much fun we are going to have, as he shows me that he is a big boy, using the potty.

I also time this with a break from work/school. One of the nice things about the society we live in, is that as a parent there are chunks of time that are given to you to be with your child (wanted or not). If you are a parent that works outside the home, you often have a winter break of at least a week (counting the weekends), a spring break, a summer break or two, and even a shorter fall break. These are wonderful times to skip the season's vacation and stay home to potty-train your child. If you are a parent who does not work outside the house, you do not need to rely on these provided chunks, but it still does help to link the potty-training with a defined time, distinct from all the time you typically spend with your child.

Although the detailed schedule I have provided worked well for me over winter break, you must establish your own mental time frame that is realistic, based on you and your child. You may look at the schedule and say, "My child doesn't need that much time." Or you may look at the schedule and say, "Uh Oh, I think my child may need more time." You are the best expert in regards to your child. You are best equipped to modify a schedule or process. One of the things that the provided schedule does is create Consistency- which potty- training cannot occur without.

2.c. Consistency

Consistency is one of the "3Cs", but what exactly does it mean? If you look up the actual American Heritage definition, you will see:

"Consistency n. 1. Agreement or logical coherence among things or parts. 2. Compatibility or agreement among successive acts, ideas, or events."

But what does this mean specifically for potty- training? From both my experience, and the limited research I have seen, a repetitive start again/stop again approach to potty-training does not have great results. If the child is ready, the good old analogy of "just rip the bandaid off already" is an example of Consistency.

The Process of potty-training must be Consistent. It does not work well for the child to learn that using the potty is optional, based on convenience or any other factor. The goal of potty-training is to teach the child that whenever he/she needs to pee or poop, it should not be in underwear or pants. Most of the time it will be in a potty, and perhaps sometimes it will be in the woods, or into a different container, e.g. an empty water bottle or plastic bag during road trips. However the Progress of the method will be able to be assessed by how much control the child exhibits over where and when elimination happens. Therefore, Consistency is crucial for the child to learn how to control when and where he/she pees and poops.

In other words in reference to the above definition, there must be both agreement between the "successive acts and events" of using the potty, as well as a "logical coherence" about the Process of using the potty.

You may be wondering about how this gets implemented in real life. For a majority of families, there is more than one caregiver interacting with a particular child. Sometimes it is an assortment of parents, grandparents, babysitters, outside the house daycare providers, and others. How is Consistency achieved with so much variation?

If you have a team of caregivers, you can still achieve Consistency by following the same schedule, and writing down any changes that you make. Communication is crucial. If you make a change, you need to share it with the next person who cares for your child, so that they can be Consistent with what you started. This will not work if one primary caregiver does not agree with the other primary caregiver about when or whether to start potty- training. (The children, young as they are, do pick up on the discord, and use it against the adults.)

Personally, although I was able to stay home with one of mine, exclusively being the one to do the potty- training, I did not have this luxury with the others. I was however always able to do the Communication leading up to the potty-training period, and the first 3 days of the schedule. After that my husband followed the schedule, as did our babysitters. Finally, with our fourth-born, I also had the issue of pre-school. My children's preschool was particularly wonderful about respecting how I was potty- training my child, and doing exactly what I asked. I am sure it was not easy for the teachers, but the reward of not having to change his diaper anymore, and of seeing how proud of himself he was, was quick to come.

As I wrote earlier, you are the best expert with regards to your child, and hence the other (non-parental) caregivers should respect your wishes and requests.

2.d. Individual personality

This aspect must also be evaluated in figuring out when to potty-train your child. It would be much easier in some ways if the children were all like little robots designed to accept programs, and the hardest thing would be to write the program correctly. However, this is just not the case. I don't need to tell you that each child has his/her own personality, with certain traits apparent from birth.

You must decide if your child's stubbornness, or declaration of independence, or desire to please you is going to hamper the potty-training process. If you start potty- training too early, your child may not be able to do it, and could feel that he/she failed. But if you wait too long to start potty- training your child, you may run into personality and temperament issues such as a battle of wills for control. Finding this window is not easy, hence it is important to note that judging incorrectly does not cause irreparable harm. I think that considering each child's individual personality and temperament is crucial. It is an easier Process if you can figure out how to interact with each particular child, such that a positive attitude can be adopted towards, and maintained during, potty- training.

Since each child-adult interaction is different, it may be hard to see how your particular situation fits in with the writings in a booklet or program. This individual-ness is one of the reasons why there is an email address provided in Chapter 6.

2.e New sibling

Another issue to take into consideration when beginning to potty-train your child is your family planning schedule. Many people talk about "the regression" that occurs after a new baby comes into the family. While this may be the case for some children, I actually think that something different is occurring for the majority of children. It just happens to be occurring at the same time. Most people have another child when the previous one is between 2 and 4 years old. This is exactly the age that young children really strive for some independence and control over their lives. Hence, they do not want to be told to go use the potty. They do not want to stop what they are playing with, and they want to do many things themselves. All of the above factors often cause children to have potty-using accidents. It also often happens to coincidentally occur when there is a new baby, puppy, job, or routine. This is not typically due to the child feeling jealous of the new baby. (Please see Chapter 6 for more information on "post potty-training issues".)

With this said, however, I have tried to potty-train my children, not while I was pregnant (too tired and too big to move quickly and comfortably), but after the next baby arrived. About a month or so after having a new baby, I was physically more comfortable, but still stuck home quite a bit. For me, this was a perfect time to use the two-week method.

If you do think that the new sibling is causing the potty- trainer to have issues, you can do at least two things. You can opt to redo the 2 week schedule listed below, or you can use your Communication tool, suggesting to your older child that he/she "teach" the baby how to use the potty. You can suggest that he/she say, "Mommy, Baby, I am going to the potty now to make pee pee/ poopy. I will tell you when I am done." Then reinforce this by telling him/her that if he/she tells you both that, and by not having accidents, this will help the baby learn, making him/her the best big brother/sister EVER.

2.f. Multiples

Anyone who has multiples, e.g. twins, triplets, jokes about the "freak show" nature of going out with the children to a store or park. I know this because my sister has twins, and has had to endure more stupid comments and stares than I ever thought could be possible. (She has handled them a lot more politely than I would have been able to. I am afraid I might have said, "Gee, did your mom forget to teach you manners, or did you really think that this could possibly be any of your business?")

Anyone who has multiples knows that many of the "self-help" child development books and techniques simply do not apply to life with multiples. Parents of multiples scan the resources looking for anything that might be relevant to the issues that arise, only to find little. They then often consult other parents of multiples, to see what others in similar situations have tried and/or found successful.

Here is what I want to say about potty-training and multiples. While I understand that much is different, I do not think that potty-training, using a two- week method is one of those things. Multiples may have been born on the same day, and shared the prenatal environment, but they are still different people. It is not inconceivable that one of the multiples may be ready to potty-train earlier than another. There is no reason why there can't be the one-to-one bond that occurs with potty-training this way, done in succession, with a two-week difference. While nothing is easy when you have two or more children of the same age, I do think it might be easier to potty-train children one at a time. In this way, you do not rush the one(s) that isn't(aren't) ready. You do not have to deal with accidents on the floor due to more than one tush trying to get to the same potty (despite there being more than one, identical, potty) at the same time. And, by staggering your potty-training, you will get better at it with each child. Parents do not change two diapers at the same exact moment, so why try to potty-train two children at the same exact time. Each child's developmental needs are different, despite being a multiple.

I think that the schedule presented in Chapter 4 can be done with multiples, and can be started whenever the parent thinks that the child is ready. Obviously, any changes made to the schedule should be noted and communicated to the other caregivers for consistency.

3 WHAT DO YOU REALLY NEED?

Okay, so you have reached this point, and you are ready to Commit to potty- training your child. What do you actually need? Again, the answer to this question is going to depend on whom you ask. If you ask your parents or grandparents, they will laugh, and probably tell you that you don't need anything. If you ask some of the younger, more technology-savvy parents, they might tell you that you need an electronic wetter device for bedtime and/or undergarments. The answer to this question is going to depend on your family's philosophy and/or own unique style. Although, regardless of philosophy and style, I do recommend you buy/have at least two, large, bleachable towels and a few rolls of paper towels. I also recommend that you have at least 3 interesting books to read to your child, as he/she sits on the potty to poop, or even just to use the potty before bed. Discussed in the rest of this chapter are the items I use/ recommend, and what some other options are, as well as some advantages and disadvantages with certain items/ideas. (Appendix 3 has an "ingredients" list. You can buy these things at stores ranging from baby-specific stores to kids' stores to Target.)

3.1 Technology

I am not sure how parents potty-trained their children without a television or computer screen to watch, but I am sure glad we have this as an option now. I don't believe in the television as an electronic babysitter, but instead as an activity to do with my child. For potty-training, I found the television and DVD-playing computer to be extremely useful.

You need to pick a potty-training video/DVD with a lot of songs that you and your child can learn to sing. It should also be between 30 and 45 minutes long. I prefer the Duke University's production, "It's Potty Time", but there are many such videos/DVDs out there. I suggest you watch through it first yourself, and decide if the songs that are taught, are the songs you want to have your child sing. I have a friend who found a video that had a song named "Accidents Happen and It's Okay". Whenever her child had an accident, he would sing that to her. That got old REALLY quickly.

I also think you need to have access to watch a movie or set of shows for a "marathon". (For some reason, my most recent 2 year old loved to watch Astroboy repeatedly. It really wasn't age- appropriate, but he saw his big brothers watching it, and begged for it.)

The potty-training video with a length of 30- 45 minutes is just the right length of time between when a new potty- trainer sits down to watch the show, and when he/she should need to pee. The longer movie, or set of shows, is designed to both hold the child's attention for a while, but still provide the child with motivation to get up, wander around, and then come back to the potty.

3.2 Location of potty seat

"… wander around, and then come back to the potty", huh? Some of you may be trying to figure out what I am talking about. Obviously you cannot move the home's regular toilets, and typically there is no TV in front of the toilet. So how can you watch a potty-training video, while sitting on the potty?

Easy (but weird, I know)- You put a child's portable potty seat on a bleachable towel on the floor directly in front of a television or computer screen. Now you are probably thinking that I am mentally "not all there". In fact, our preschool director thinks it is totally gross, and she is not often wrong. It is okay to feel that way. I know it sounds odd, but I promise this is not permanent. For the first two weeks of potty- training, it is helpful to have the potty seat in front of the television/computer screen. After your child gets more used to both using the potty and recognizing the urges to use the potty, the potty seat can be moved to the bathroom, next to the "big" potty. Finally, it gets moved out of the house, as your child will have transitioned to using only the regular toilet. (We have always thrown them out after each child, not wanting to keep them. But you could decide to try to find a way to wash them well, and to keep them for future siblings.)

The advantage of treating the potty seat as a new toy and as part of a new activity, i.e. watching TV while peeing, is that it is novel and fun. Hence, the children seem to want to "play" the potty-training game. The disadvantage is that if the child misses the potty and the towel, your floor gets wet.

I have always set the potty and towel up in the room where there was both a television and a lot of toys. The TV did not always hold the child's attention, so the toys often broke up the time, while still keeping him near the potty seat.

Many people put the portable potty seat in the regular bathroom, so that the child can do the same thing the adult is doing, just on a potty seat sized for children. I have not had much success with doing that. I have found that when the kids were just starting to potty-train, they would not pee completely, and would pee every time they felt they had a drop to put in. Therefore, they would spend a lot of time on and near the potty seat. The regular bathroom is boring and small, hence the kids did not want to stay in there for long. Neither did I for that matter.

3.3 Type of potty seat

When you go to the store to look for a potty seat, you may be confronted with more choices than you thought could even be possible.

There are ones that are thin and attach to your normal toilet seat. There are those that have handles on the side and sit right inside your normal toilet seat. There are those that are on their own base such that they can convert to a stepstool when turned upside down. More still, there are those that look like chairs and thrones. There are those that play music, and those that give applause. There are blue ones, and pink ones, and green, yellow, and purple ones. At this point you can find a potty seat that can do everything- short of potty-train your child, that is.

Potty seats range in price from approximately $10 to approximately $75. You need to choose the one that you think best suits your child. I have always chosen a potty seat based on the particular child I was training. One of my children loved hearing the song play after he peed in the potty. Another would have gotten scared, jumped off, and run away. Another would take apart any potty seat we brought in, hence the fewer parts the better. The two most important aspects of the potty seat for this method are portability and ease of emptying it. (Some people argue that it also has to be easy for the child to empty him/herself. I never allowed my children to empty it themselves because I didn't want them to spill it anywhere.) It needs to be able to be moved, so that it can be set in front of the television/computer screen, and then later moved to the bathroom. It needs to be easy to empty and clean, since you will frequently be doing that. One of my children would trickle a bit, and then want me to empty it into the big potty. He liked to watch as I flushed. Which specific potty seat you decide to buy should depend on your own child's personality, and how much you want to spend on it.

3.4 Pull-ups and underwear

Many people have asked me about using something like Pull-ups and/or underwear. It helps to have one package of daytime pull-ups, and a large package of nighttime pull-ups. For this method, pull-ups are used for about 2 weeks, after the child is not so new to potty-training. I do not recommend using them as if they were diapers. It sends the wrong message, regarding Consistency, for achieving the goal of putting all pee-pee and poopy in the potty. The exception to this is night time. It is very difficult for many young children to potty-train at night in the same way they do during the day because they are asleep and can't recognize the urges. Therefore, if you say to the child, "No more diapers", then putting diapers on them at night is not only inconsistent, but also can make the child feel like he/she has failed. You can however, say to the child, "Now that we are done with diapers, you get to wear these great big kid pull-ups." Until a child can be dry through the night, using nighttime pull-ups is fine. For many kids, night-time potty use is very variable and being encouraging/ supportive is best.

Many people use underwear as a reward. The problem with this is that if your child does have an accident and you "punish" the behavior by taking away the underwear, you are cutting your nose off to spite your face. What now? If you take away the child's underwear, you need to put them in something, right? But you certainly don't want to go back to a diaper, just because the child had an accident. I don't recommend using underwear as a reward, or even as an incentive. It can be difficult for children to understand why underwear is an incentive for them to complete a Process that is challenging. I do recommend buying a package of underwear that you think your child will enjoy wearing. I also recommend encouraging your child by showing him/her the underwear you chose, saying, "When you know how and when to use the potty, you will get to wear these under your clothing. Isn't that great?!".

You can choose from boxers and briefs for boys, and from the different options for girls as well. Underwear comes in all different colors, with different characters and designs. It is important to try to size it appropriately, as you want the underwear to be comfortable for the child. Along the lines of keeping the child comfortable, I have also found it helpful to buy sweatpants and/or other bottoms with an elastic waistband. You want to enable your child to succeed independently. With an elastic waistband, the child can pull up and down his/her pants or shorts, even in a hurry. With buttons or snaps, this task is more difficult and stressful.

3.5 Rewards

I have already discussed the use of underwear as a reward, and how I don't recommend it. There are several other things that many people use, but I do not. I do not suggest using food, like candy/M&Ms as a reward for using the potty. Been there, done that! I was advised by many reputable people and professionals to use M&Ms. Oh boy was that a problem. I was reminded by my 19 month old that children are smart. They will figure out that the more times they go to the potty, the more treats they will get. Therefore, they may not void completely, so that they can get more candy. This reward system does not lead to self-confidence, self-motivation, or pride. It also quickly becomes both a negative aspect, and a hindrance to potty-training. It leads to more arguments between the child and adult as the children try to argue for more candy.

Unfortunately, stickers can be the same way. If you reward the child with a sticker each time he/she uses the potty, you have the same situation as with the candy. If you decide to use a sticker chart at the end of the day, you are asking a young child to accept a delayed gratification. This is often difficult.

So what do I use instead? This is where Commendation comes in, and works beautifully. Children really do respond to verbal praise with eye contact. The more you talk with your child about how well he/she is doing, the more rewarded the child feels, and the more eager the child is to continue. I also use a high five, or other type of gesture. If you think about it, even adults smile a little bigger when they are told, sincerely, that they are doing well with something.

The other reward I recommend is offering to let the child flush the potty him/herself, once you do empty it (or on the big potty, if that's where your child is at in the Process.)

Again the main reason to reward the child for using the potty is for him/her to want to continue using it. This is even more crucial than just having the child use it.

21

3.6 Clothing Choices

I mentioned in section 3.4 the benefits of sweatpants, but there is a bit more to consider. Clothing can help and/or hinder a child's attempts to use the potty. When you are potty-training, think easy up and easy down. Overalls should be discarded! There is little worse for a young, potty- training child than overalls, with straps and snaps. Also on the "no-no list" are tights, button pants, one-piece zipper front pajamas, long dresses/shirts that can get dipped into the potty, or need to be held up. Wardrobe choices, while still fashionable, like "jeggings" for girls and elastic waist slacks for boys, must be considered carefully for both up/down ease and independence.

For night time potty-training, which often happens a number of months after day time potty-training begins, pajamas that snap the top to the bottoms are often quite difficult for young children.

3.7 Timers

I do not recommend egg timers, or any other timer. Although I do tell you that you should remind your child to use the potty, it should always be an approximation. When a timer is used, I have seen a few things happen. The first is that the child grows to hate the timer. The second is that the child does not pay attention to his/her own body's signal, but instead waits for the timer. The third is that the adult leaves the room and stops Communication and Commendation, which are both important parts of the Process.

It is okay if you are not "timer precise" with reminding your child to use the potty. At some point soon, you want your child to recognize his/her own urges- without a bell!

4 HOW TO ACTUALLY POTTY-TRAIN: THE SCHEDULE

4.1 Things to consider:

I mentioned earlier that there are some gender differences that, while perhaps not important to *when* to potty-train, are important for *how* to potty-train. The ability to stand to pee is one of these differences. Girls are taught to pee while sitting, and it still trickles everywhere, especially if they are not reminded to lean forward a bit. Boys, theoretically, can be taught to pee either sitting or standing. (Although they must sit on the potty to poop.)

Believe it or not, this is a loaded topic. For some reason, many men feel their masculinity challenged if they sit to pee, despi   e fact that their aim is rarely accurate and most women never think about it at all. Our personal, house rule is that in the house or any other clean bathroom, the boys sit to pee. Outside of a clean or familiar bathroom, they should stand to pee. Our boys can pee both ways without a problem. More importantly they do not leave a mess for anyone at play dates or at home, AND no one falls into the potty because the seat was accidentally left up. This is especially useful for when there are younger children around.

Regardless of how you end up dealing with the sitting/standing debate with potty-trained boys, they should all start sitting. The immediate goal is not to teach them to aim for cheerios in the potty, but to recognize the urge to pee/poop, as well as the sensation of not needing to pee/poop anymore. This is best learned while sitting.

The other thing I learned about potty-training boys is that anatomically, when little boys pee, their penis goes up. Girls trickle down, and boys shoot upwards. Having only had a sister, I was not aware of this. I had to clean the ceiling and the walls until I realized this, and learned that I needed to teach the boys to point it down into the potty before peeing. My sister, who has twin girls, has had to clean the front of the toilet, when the girls decided to recline while peeing.

One more thought is on toilet paper and the child wiping him/herself. For boys, I recommend wiping them or double-checking their wiping until approximately age 5 years. Same for girls with poopie. I think that for girls wiping after peeing, it depends on when they can understand about using no more than 3 squares of toilet paper. This is not just about Communication, but also about not wanting the child to fall off the potty while reaching for the paper, or when wiping him/herself. The fall could be a bit traumatic, and a deterrent for Consistent use. Just as importantly, the child needs to be clean after using the bathroom. Hmm, a side note on wiping: We have always had the children lean forward and hold on to our legs, as we wipe them from behind. We have found this the best way to get them clean, not have their fingers anywhere they should not be, and the children hold on, so they do not feel like they will fall off the potty.

4.2   How to start:

Remember the 3 Cs and the 3 Pros; Communication, Consistency, and Commendation; Process, Progress, and Problems. For successful potty-training, talking about it before you begin is really helpful. As you start, try to time it with the ending of a pack of diapers. Show the end of the diapers, with the diapers disappearing one at a time from the package. Talk about becoming a big kid, and all the wonderful things that you can do when you wear big kid underwear. Also plan on starting such that you time potty- training with a weekend before a week-long break from work, school, or other activities.

Plan on having enough food and necessities for the first week of potty-training. If you follow the proposed schedule, you will be stuck in the house for almost the whole week, with a bare bottomed child. But this is not meant to be negative. It is time that you will rarely have again. Enjoy the challenge you both will have, and the time spent together.

- o **Detailed Schedule** (Please see the visual timeline for quick review and easy use, at the end of this chapter.)
  - ▪ Day 1 (Preferably a Friday night): Normal day with diaper, but say, "Tonight we will sit on the potty while we brush your teeth. Isn't that exciting?" Before bed, take off the diaper, sit your child on the potty. Give him/her a moist toothbrush (no toothpaste) and let him/her brush teeth, sitting on the potty, while you read a book to him/her.
  - ▪ Day 2: Wake child up, about 5 minutes earlier than usual. If the diaper isn't dirty, take off the diaper, happily saying, "Let's go sit on the potty!!" Then ask which potty your child wants to sit on- either the big potty, where teeth were brushed or the potty seat in front of the tv.
    - • If your child is sitting in front of the tv, put on your potty video.
    - • Most of your day today will be watching movies and doing other activities with a bare-bottomed child near the potty.
    - • Praise your child, verbally, every time pee-pee makes it into the potty. Shake your head, "No" when the child doesn't get it in, and ask, "Where does pee pee go? Where does poopie go?" Your child should answer, "in the potty". If your child can't say it, or point to the potty, he/she may be too young.
    - • Do not put a diaper, pull-up, or underwear on your child today. If that means that meals are consumed near the potty, it is okay. Two days of an eating routine-change should not devastate the child, especially if the whole goal is a change away from diapers. (There is obviously change to the

25

routine anyway, with trying to use the potty instead of diapers.)

- Before bed, the same routine is followed with the toothbrush, big potty, and books. For overnight, put on a night-time pull-up, saying, "You did such a good job trying to use the potty today that you get to wear a big kid, night-time pull-up! Good job! I can't wait to do it all again tomorrow."

■ Day 3: Much like yesterday, wake child up, happily remind child about using the potty, and ask which one he/she wants to sit on first. Your goal is to establish a new routine of using the potty upon waking up.

- Your child should watch your selected how-to-potty video at least twice per day. This reinforces that other children use the potty, and typically has "how-to" songs that you can sing with your child, when he/she uses the real potty.
- Your child should be less interested in the tv today. Encourage your child to try to use the potty every 5- 10 minutes. Praise, verbally, for trying and for success. Just calmly say, "No", for accidents. Do NOT have your child "help" you clean up their accidents. They are not dogs that should have their noses wiped in it. At this stage, they are new learners, not spiteful messmakers. They should not be scolded, yelled at, punished, or have things taken away. After they have been potty-trained for a few months, some of this can be reconsidered. See Chapter 6 for more on this.)
- Again, today is a bare-bottom day. All activities should be bare- bottomed and near the potty.
- Before bed, follow the same routine as the previous days. Your goal is to establish the routine of using the potty before going to sleep.

■ Day 4: Would you be surprised, if I wrote, follow the same morning routine of the past few days? Probably not. By now, if your child is ready to be potty-trained, there should be the beginning of eagerness to go use the potty, on the child's part.

- While today is still a bare bottom day, you should be noticing that your child is actually allowing more urine out at a time, and starting to "hold it" until he/she is on the potty. You should also notice if your child is pooping on the potty, or trying to wait for a diaper or pull-up. This is

common. See Chapter 5: Common concerns, potential solutions
- This is an intense week, but the end result is worth it. Keep going.
- You, the adult will be very bored of this, and might even think of stopping. Keep going. One week of consistency and boredom is worth not needing to buy diapers again.
- Do not put a pull-up on and go out to do an errand, no matter how well your child seems to be doing!
- Follow the same night-time routine.

- Days 5 and 6:
  - Exactly the same as Days 2-4. By now you are ALL sick of the potty, the videos, and the bare bottom. But you should see that your child is doing a great job. Keep going.
    - Tell your child that tomorrow you are going to run an errand together, and that he/she will get to wear a pull-up.
    - Same night time routine.

- Day 7: Hurray, the big day!
  - Same morning routine.
  - After the second successful pee pee following food or drink, quickly get your child dressed in a pull-up (or underwear if you are really brave), sweatpants, and a loose-fitting shirt. Have everyone who is going on the outing try to use the potty one more time, then out you go.
    - o Where to go? I recommend a store or park that has a clean(ish) bathroom that is easily accessible.
  - After 20 minutes, say, "It's time to find a potty! Let's go on a search for the potty, and when we find it, you can try it!". Be positive and upbeat. Pretend to look for it, but really get there kind of quickly.
  - Have your child try to use the potty. Hopefully the pull-up/ underwear will be dry, and the child will be able to pee a bit in the potty there. Regardless, praise your child for the attempt.

- Time your outing such that you are home 20 minutes after the outing's potty attempt.
- Try the potty again at your home.
- At this point, if your outing was a success, keep a pull up or underwear on your child (not needing a bare bottom constantly). BUT remind your child to use the potty every 10 minutes. Sometimes your child will go, and sometimes not. Your child needs to learn to recognize his/her own urges.
- If your outing was not a success, don't worry. There will be more outings. Go back to the bare-bottom, movie watching process (for 3 more days. Then try another outing). Do not give up!

- Day 8: If you started on a Friday, it is Friday again. You may be feeling pressure about getting your child "school"-ready by Monday. Don't fret. You should be through the worst of it.
  - Keep the morning routine the same.
  - Try a pull-up (or underwear) and sweatpants in the home.
  - Remind your child to try to use the potty, every 20 minutes or so. If the undergarment stays dry, keep going this way. You might even try another outing.
  - If the undergarment gets wet, try again with a new undergarment, but remind him/her to try to use the potty every 10 minutes.
  - Verbally reward often.
  - Keep the bedtime routine the same.

- Day 9: Your goal today is to have your child in dry undergarments the whole day, while reducing the reminders to every 30 minutes.
  - Morning routine is the same.
  - Daytime routine should now include putting on an undergarment and sweatpants after using the potty upon waking.
  - Hopefully, your child is now starting to tell you on his/her own when he/she needs to use the potty. Try encouraging him/her to use different potties in the home.
  - Try to go on two short outings today.
  - For bedtime, see if you can separate tooth-brushing from sitting on the potty. Say, "Okay, do you want to brush your teeth before you use the potty tonight?". If the child fights it, just say,

"That's fine. It is your choice. Perhaps
tomorrow you will choose to brush your teeth
first."

- Day 10: Your goal is to reinforce your child's "good
choices" to use the potty, keep undergarments dry, use
words to tell you that he/she needs to use the potty, and
any other act of independence, e.g. washing hands,
pulling up pants, etc.
    - By now, if you have put all of the intensive work
    into the cause of potty-training, and are seeing no
    result, it is okay to acknowledge that your child is
    not ready yet. Not every child is ready to potty-
    train at the same time. Congratulate your child
    and yourself for a GREAT effort, and put this
    booklet away until your child is ready.
    - If your child seems just about potty-trained, please
    realize that you have the basics down, but there
    might be accidents and regressions for another few
    months. Your goal is to use the next 4 days to
    encourage your independent child to make good
    potty choices.
    - Keep going with the morning and night-time
    routine. Keep going with suggesting your child use
    the potty before you leave the home and after
    you return to the home.
    - When you see your child is REALLY involved in
    playing with a toy, try interrupting him/her to use
    the potty. Your child needs to learn that the
    interesting toy or activity will still be there when
    he/ she returns. (See Chapter 5, problems for more
    on this.)
- Days 11-14: If your child is home with you, keep going
with the routines. Go on longer and longer outings. If
your child is at "school", make sure you tell the adults to
take him/ her to the bathroom every 20 minutes, then 30
minutes, then 45 minutes. This needs to be done until
the child is comfortable using the new potty, in the new
place, with new people. After 3 days or so, it should be
more like at home.

    o Hooray! You are here!

- At this point, you are either thrilled to pieces that the worst is over, and whatever comes up, you know how to handle it, OR you have learned that your child is not quite ready yet. Both of these possibilities are fine. You must allow for individual variation. Do not ever tell the child that he/she failed. Do not ever tell yourself that you failed. You have a specific set of instructions to follow for when you think you are both ready to try again.

- At this point, you may have questions or concerns that have come up. Please see the next chapter to see if they are covered there.

- At this point, if your child is successfully potty-trained during the day, you may be wondering what you are supposed to do for night-time potty-training. Please see Chapter 7.

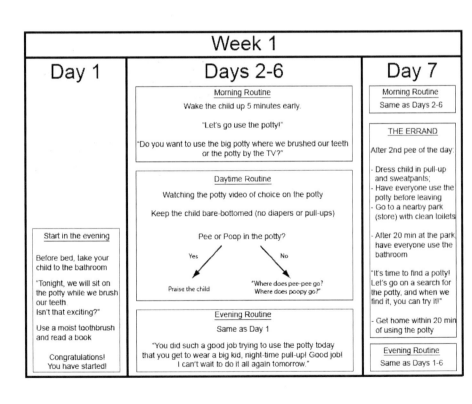

Week 2

Day 8	Day 9	Day 10	Days 11-14
Morning Routine Same as Week 1	**Morning Routine** Same as Week 1	**Morning Routine** Same as Week 1	**Morning Routine** Same as Week 1
Daytime Routine Pull-up or underwear with sweatpants all day Reminder every 20 min If child stays dry, keep going If he/she gets it wet, change underwear and remind every 10 min Consider a short outing Frequent verbal rewards	**Daytime Routine** An undergarment with sweatpants all day Reminder every 30 min Encourage child to tell you if he/she has to go Encourage child to use different potties at home Attempt 2 short outings Frequent verbal rewards	**Daytime Routine** Reinforce child's "good choices": - to use the potty - to keep underwear dry - to use words to tell you he/she has to go - to be independent, e.g. wash hands, pull up his/her pants Redirect child towards the potty when he/she is involved with a toy for prolonged time	**Daytime Routine at Home** Keep going!!! Attempt longer and longer trips **Daytime Routine at School** Instruct caregivers to take the child to the bathroom - every 20 minutes on day 11 - every 30 minutes on day 12 - every 45 minutes on days 13-14 Keep the reminders at school going until child can express his/her urges and is comfortable using the potty at school
	Evening Routine Attempt to separate tooth-brushing from sitting on the potty "Do you want to brush your teeth before you sit on the potty?"		
Evening Routine Same as Week 1		**Evening Routine** Same as Day 9	**Evening Routine** Same as Day 9

5 COMMON CONCERNS, POTENTIAL SOLUTIONS

There are numerous concerns, problems, and issues that people who are potty-training children face. Some of them are covered in this chapter. However, I know that there are many more. Often times, just when you think the potty-training is going well, you have a "Yikes, what now?" period. These are often difficult to deal with.

5.1 Not wanting to get off the potty

This seems like such a silly concern after your child has been potty- trained for years, however when you are going through the Process, it can be quite frustrating. There are a number of reasons for why a potty-training child may not want to get off the potty. Some of these reasons fall within the range of: the child may not recognize the urge and doesn't want to have an accident; the child may be enjoying the attention focused on him/her while he/she is on the potty and is afraid that the attention will stop, or the child knows that you want him/her off and is trying to engage you in a power struggle.

If the reason is of biological need/awareness, the response is to let the child be, and continue Commending/ supporting him/her. He/She will not stay on the potty forever. There are too many other interesting things to do and see. This is one of the reasons why I wrote that you should be prepared to spend a lot of time in the house together for the first period of potty-training.

If the reason is of enjoying the attention, you can redirect the child, while maintaining the same high level of attention. For example, you can say, "I am soooo proud of how well you are using the potty. Now that you are such a big boy/girl, do you want to play a game together? Let's go pick it out. We can always come back to the potty when you need to use it again." (Follow- through is also important, so do make sure to return to the previous activity.)

If the reason is one of control, and need for independent decision making, the first thing to try is quite different than what I recommend for the other situations. The age/stage of potty-training often coincides with the stage of the child wanting to feel like he/she has some control over his/her life and actions. I do recommend giving the child choices, but not with a "yes"/ "no" answer. For example, if the child says, "I am not getting off this potty.", I would suggest you say, "Okay. Are you going to be finished using the potty, and getting off on your own, in 1 minute or 3 minutes?"

In this way, you are acknowledging that the child is going to get off the potty by him/herself, but the choice is when, not whether. If the child says, "3 minutes", and still doesn't get off, then you have another problem. You do not want to pull the child off, and associate the potty with a negative experience. (I know that is easy to say/write, and I would be lying if I wrote that I have never pulled any of my children off the potty in this situation. But do try to find another way, saving the "YOU'RE DONE!!" language and actions for a last resort.) I have provided a list of things that you can try to say when it becomes a battle of control in Appendix 4. They may not work, but they might help you figure out something that you can modify to use with your own child.

5.2 Constipation

It is very common for children to get the hang of peeing in the potty before pooping in the potty. It is also very common for children to not want to poop in the potty, holding out for a diaper. When they do this, it often leads to constipation. I have asked my children why pooping in the potty is so different. I have been lucky enough to get three different responses from 3 of my 4 children. My most recent potty-training child said that pooping in the potty hurts. One of my older boys said that he didn't want to get splashed with cold, yucky water. And another of my older boys said that he remembered that it was scary.

There are a number of things you can do to help with this problem. The best thing you can do is loosen and soften up the poop by giving your child extra fiber through fruit and vegetables. If this doesn't work, you should call your pediatrician to ask about adding something like Miralax or Lactulose to the child's drink in the morning. (My children call it "poopie medicine", and will drink a teaspoon of Lactulose right from a spoon.). By making it easier for the child to poop, it eliminates some of the fear and pain. If a child is truly inconsolable, it makes more sense to give the child a diaper to poop in, then to risk him/her keeping it in and getting sick. Continue to encourage the child to pee in the potty, and just keep talking about how wonderful it will be when he/she is comfortable pooping in the potty too.

One of the things you don't want to do, is pressure your child to poop in the potty before he/she is ready. Anything negative, or attention-calling to this aspect of potty use, typically finds the child taking longer. It often feels like this aspect will never happen, but it will. Just keep with the positive outlook, and Commendation.

5.3 Illness

Many people notice that when their children are sick with a cold or virus, they do not use the potty as successfully. This is fine. If you are thinking about potty-training, and your child gets sick, it is better to wait for him/her to be healthy. If you have already been working on potty-training, and your child gets sick, just realize that there might be more accidents, and it might take longer. Other than to remind your child more frequently to try to use the potty, there isn't much you can do. Remember to Commend your child frequently!

5.4 Fear of the flush/fear of "unfamiliar" potties

Some children love being able to flush the potty. Others hate the noise of the toilet flushing. This can be extremely difficult when you take your child to a potty at a store or restaurant, and it is an automatically flushing potty. Normally these toilets are activated by changes in light or movement. If you find that the only available potty is an automatic flusher, you can use your hand or a piece of toilet paper, to cover the sensor until your child has finished using the potty and is far enough away. Just make sure to tell your child what to expect, so that the noise is not a true startling surprise. Some parents tell their child to cover his/ her ears. I could not do that with my children, because they were afraid of falling in if their hands weren't propping themselves up.

Some children are tearful of potties they don't know, which is difficult to deal with if you go to a store, restaurant, school, or even a friend's house. This is where Communication remains an important aspect. While you are talking to your child about using the potty, or even if you are just playing with different color/shape toys, you can discuss that potties come in all kinds of exciting colors, shapes, and heights. Explain that some are white, and some are green, blue, or pink. Explain that some are close to the ground, and others are high up, like a throne. Tell your child that the different potties may sound a little different too. Explain that even though they may look and sound different, they are all very similar. You can then offer to go on a "potty safari", next time you go out to see how many different types and colors of potties you can "spot" and try to use.

5.5 Using the potty is not exciting anymore

So what happens when the potty is not exciting anymore? When it is not a novel game that attracts attention? This is often a turning point for parents. The kids lose interest in the potty and the parents/adults put a diaper or pull-up back on the child. My recommendation is different. If your child has shown the ability to use the potty, do not put him/her back in diapers or a pull-up. Talk to your child more. Do the opposite. Tell your child that you are not packing an extra pair of underwear and pants, so he/she must put all poopy and pee pee in the potty that day.

You can also try a different set of movies- both potty- training and general watching. See if that causes more interest. Without getting angry at your child, realize that we, even as adults, find using the potty to be something we have to do that is bordering on wasting time that we have to do other things. We can't expect our children to always find it exciting. It is important to respond to the child positively and praise him/her for using the potty so that he/she can do other really cool "big kid" things. (More on this will be addressed in Chapter 6 as well.)

5.6 What counts as an accident?

Okay, when your child has been peeing so well in the potty, but now is having "accidents", are all accidents equal? The answer to this question is no. If the child drenches his/her underwear, and didn't realize that he/she had to pee, it is different than just a "pee spot".

It is not uncommon for children, especially boys, to pee a little bit, feel the cold, wet on the tip of their penis, and then hold the rest of it as they dash to the bathroom. This should not count as a true accident, but instead as part of the advanced learning process. The kids may ask for new underwear or pants, but it is not necessary. It will dry. You can change them if you want. The important thing to note is that this "pee spot" will stop happening as your child gets older. The fact that it is not a full drenching already means that your child is potty-training. Just keep going. Instead of being angry at him/her, make sure to say how proud of him/her you are for getting to the potty and for getting most of the pee pee in the potty.

Another "non-accident" is when the child is on antibiotics or other medicines and "toots", with some poop getting in the underwear. It is important to clean up and change the child, saying that it is not his/her fault, but probably the medicine that is so important to his/her feeling better otherwise. Most "brown streaks" are not accidents, but the result of not being wiped well enough. Hence, these too, do not count as accidents. The child should be reassured of this, if he/she is concerned.

Yet other "non-accidents" include when the child makes it to the potty, but there is some dripping on the pants, or when the child tells the caregiver, but the caregiver does not get the child to the potty on time. In both of these situations, it is quite understandable that the child and parent/caregiver would be upset. However, continue telling the child how wonderful he/she is doing, getting better every day.

5.7 We already started with a different method

Many parents will reach for this, or any of the other potty-training books after first trying their own way or even a different method. However not every method works for every child. If the other way of potty-training did not work, how do you start again? At what point do you pick up from what is written here, for example?

Two situations that normally occur are when a parent says, "I am going to pick up from where I think my child is.", and "My child is way too advanced for this method, so I am not going to try it from the beginning."

I think that while well-intentioned, these reactions set the child up for failure. Even if the child sometimes uses the real potty, but just not reliably, it does not mean that you can't start from the beginning. Children play in pretend kitchens and even real kitchens sometimes. This does not mean that they know how to cook. It is perfectly reasonable to say to your child, "I am so proud of you for how you use the big potty. Now we are going to have fun learning WHEN to use the potty. We are going to do this with a potty that is just your size. We are going to have so much fun."

By starting the Process, with open Communication in this fashion, you are not taking anything away from your child. You are still being encouraging. And, if your child has used the "big" potty, it may not take as long to learn.

6 BEYOND THE BASICS

At this point, if you have gotten through the two(ish) weeks and you are now diaper free, you are probably feeling pretty good. Perhaps even feeling like it was kind of easy. You should definitely feel pleased, but also keep in mind that you may be in a "calm before the storm" period. Potty-using is a Process that takes up to a year to fully master.

It is not uncommon for children who potty-trained successfully from the start to have accidents throughout the day about a month or so after they are "potty- trained". It is frustrating because you know they are having accidents even though they KNOW how to use the potty, and that pee pee and poopy should only go there. It is not uncommon for parents to start getting "advice" from well- meaning parents, teachers, and strangers.

Before you slide back and put the child in diapers or a pull-up again, try to figure out why the child is having accidents. The children do have the basics of potty-training, so what now? There are several reasons for why your child might be having accidents at this point. I am going to present a few of them here. I am sure there are more. Just remember that no matter what any well-meaning advise-giver says, you are doing a great job, and you will figure it out. Keep going forward.

6.1 The Upper Limit

Now that your child has learned to recognize the urge to pee/poop, and how to use the potty, he/she is probably feeling comfortable with the Process. He/she may be starting to return focus to playing, and other activities. This is good, and is exactly what you want. However, it is also common for many accidents to happen, as the child learns just how long he/she can wait. Often times this upper limit occurs because the child waited too long.

There are a few things you can try, to help your child through this time. First, you should remind your child every 30 minutes to listen to his/her body, and to think about whether he/she should try to use the potty. Second, you should have a discussion with your child about "pausing the game" for a potty break. I have paused movies, meals, games, and so on, for my potty- trainer to see that listening to his body AND using his words will help him play better and drier. A third thing you can do is to tell him/her, when small accidents happen, that it is okay, and that he/she should get to the potty a little earlier next time.

It is important to realize that even as adults, we sometimes "hold it" for as long as we can so that we can finish doing something. Children do the same thing sometimes.

6.2 Stubborn takes over

Now that your child is most likely producing and comprehending more, language-wise, and he/she is more independent, you may notice that your child may be a bit more stubborn than before. You might suggest that he/she go use the potty, and in response you may get a defiant, "No!"

This may happen not just with using the potty, but with other things as well. When it is in regards to using the potty, there are a number of things you can try. The success of some of these will depend on the particular child. One that does not depend on the child is in regards to "house rule". It should be a house rule for every member of the family to try to use the potty right before leaving the house, and perhaps right upon returning. With the house rule in effect, it s not a question, nor is it a power issue: Everyone gets dressed before leaving, and everyone uses the potty.

Other things you can try include:

Counting to 3, i.e. saying to the child, "When I count to three you need to be heading to the bathroom, one ... two ... three."

Making it a race, i.e. saying to the child, "Who is going to make it to the potty first, you or me?" (and then pretend to start racing, always allowing him/her to win)

Setting a timer, i.e. saying to the child, "In 3 minutes, when you hear the ding, you must try to use the potty." (I have not found this to work for long.)

Allowing the child a choice, i.e. telling the child, "Do you want to go try to use the potty in 3 minutes or 5 minutes?"

Allowing the child the ability to say for him/herself that he/ she needs to go to the bathroom. i.e. saying to the child, "I would like you to use the bathroom now, but you know when your body has to go, right? You can tell me that you have to use the potty now. When you go, please tell me if you need help with the light or anything else." (If this seems to be working, but you need a little more, you can then add, "Do you want to go check if the light is on, or if you will need any help in there?")

6.3. Uncertainty

If you are really not sure what is going on with your child, and the accidents, there are two things you can do. If you think it is biologically- related, you should call your pediatrician. If you think it is that your child has forgotten what to do, you can keep him/her home for 2 days, watching the potty- training video and singing the songs. It will come back to your child quickly. If you think it is that your child has been drinking a lot more liquids since it is hot outside, or that you think your child is not communicating with a caregiver, try to fix these things one at a time. Communicate with your child. Tell him/ her that drinking water is good, but when you drink more water you have to pee more, and that this is okay. Tell your child that even though he/she might be with a new teacher/ babysitter/ caregiver, it is still important to tell them in enough time to get to the potty.

6.4 Regressing

If your child starts having more frequent accidents up to around 6 months after potty-training, it often feels like he/she is regressing. This is not necessarily the case. It is important to ask him/her if he/she knows where pee pee and poopy go. This reminder reinforces both what the child knows and does. It also maintains the Communication that is so important for young children. It is also okay to ask the child why he or she had an accident. You my get answers ranging from, "I don't know" to "The potty was too far away".

If these verbal reminders don't seem to work, it is okay to keep the child home for a day, bare-bottomed, needing to show the consistent use of the potty in order to get underwear back. Typically, by this point, children want to wear their underwear. They will work hard to get it back.

7 NIGHT TIME POTTY-TRAINING

Okay, the day time potty-training accidents are able to be mediated. What about night-time potty-training? Night-time potty-training is very different from day time potty-training. During the night, children are asleep, and even if they can recognize the urge, it is hard for them to wake up fully, go to the potty, and then go back to bed. (Not to mention that the sound of the toilet flushing often wakes them up further.)

Provided below is a "how-to", with useful tips and suggestions, for night time potty-training. However, young children must be potty-trained during the day before night time potty-training can be successful. They must also have enough language to understand when you tell them that you will help them use the potty at night. The child must understand that he/she does not have to wake up fully, but does have to let you help him/her. And, just as importantly, there must be Consistency in an adult taking the child to the potty late at night-every night.

7.1 Night-time potty-training

- So, now you are feeling pretty good about the daytime potty-training. Your child uses the potty regularly with few accidents. But what about the long period at night? You might be wondering how this works. Well here, in this chapter, are some things for you to consider. First, you must remember that the children are still young, with little bladders. It is best to use pull-ups until your child is able to get up out of bed and go to the bathroom safely, in the middle of the night. If your child is still in a crib, it is not feasible to expect him/her to be potty-trained at night. This does not mean take him/her out of the crib sooner than you are ready. It means you need to have a little patience until you and your child are ready to say goodbye to the crib.

- In the meantime, there are some ways of preparing for nighttime potty-training. Much of the following information can be done whether your child is in a crib or a bed. The first of which is make sure your child is well hydrated during the day. If your child drinks enough during the day, you can get rid of the sippy cup or bottle after dinner/ before bed. If your child is well hydrated, it is a good idea to limit liquid consumption after dinner. If you give a child a cup of water or milk right before bed, guess what is going to happen? That's right. It needs to come out. Try to reduce liquid consumption after dinner steadily, until your child is not drinking much for up to 2 hours before bed.
- Make sitting on the potty part of the bedtime ritual. Read a book to your child while he/she is sitting on the potty, in order to give your child the longest chance to fully empty his/her bladder.
- At the same time, if your child goes to sleep at about 8:00pm, gently pick him/her up out of his bed at about 11:00 and put him/her on the potty. He/She should groggily pee and then go right back to sleep. Do not turn on all of the lights. Keep your voice to a whisper, as you tell him/her that he/she is going to quickly try to use the potty before going right back to sleep. Do not bother with hand washing, or even loud flushing. (You can flush after you put your child back in his/her bed.)
- Although this is a bit cumbersome for you at first, it will help establish a routine such that your child learns to wake up just enough to use the bathroom, and then return to sleep. By doing it at 11:00pm, it should make it better for you once the child is doing it on his/her own. If he/she needs you, better at 11:00pm than 3:00 in the morning.
- Once your child has up to a week of a dry pull-up in the morning, you can try to switch to underwear. Please remember that no one is perfect, and even still your child may have an occasional accident until he/she is 6 years old.

43

- Once you switch to underwear, I recommend that you put a protective surface on the child's mattress, until he/she is old enough such that accidents no longer happen.

7.2 Night-time Crying

As your child becomes potty- trained at night, it is not uncommon for crying and screaming spells in the middle of the night. Often these situations are confused with nightmares, but for the potty-training child it could instead be that he/she needs to pee. If your child starts crying or screaming, gently tell your child that you are going to carry him/her to the potty. Reassure your child that everything is okay, and that soon he/she will be back asleep.

7.3 Refusing to Go to the Potty

It is often the case that a child might groggily say, "No, I don't need to go. I want to sleep." If this happens, you can tell your child that you know that he/she may not have to go, but his/her body might want to try. Then tell him/her that he/she doesn't need to wake up, and that you will do all of the work. This sounds corny, but it does work.

If your child insists that he/she doesn't have to go, and he/she is normally dry through the night, you can say, "Okay, thank you for telling me", and see what happens in the morning. It might be that he/she truly doesn't have to pee.

7.4 In closing

Potty-training, while attempted for over 2 million children per year in the United States alone, is still an under-informed Process. There are more popular books on birthing and nursing than there are on potty-training. As a result, many people are forced to "recreate the wheel", instead of being able to successfully learn from what others have tried. It is still very common for someone to say, "That method would never work for my child." This leads to parents feeling isolated and overwhelmed.

The "3Cs" and the "3Pros" (Communication, Consistency, and Commending and the Process, the Progress, and the Problems), should hopefully be the start of ending this isolation and sentiment, making potty-training a happier stage/time. This booklet is a work in progress. I hope in the future to add more, and create a second edition based on feedback I get from parents who try this approach and respond to me. Please remember that as your child's parent and/or caregiver, you are the best expert for your child.

In attempt to facilitate a second edition, but more importantly in trying to be most helpful to parents, I can be reached at Potty.pros@aol.com. I will check this email address approximately 3 times per week on average, and will reply. I think that when you are going through the Process, sometimes it helps to write out exactly what your child is doing, and how you are handling it. Sometimes you may be able to figure out how to fix the Problem yourself, after reading what you wrote. Sometimes, having someone else respond to your unique situation is also comforting, if not helpful. I may not always have the right answer, but having two people working on the issue is often better than one.

References

American Heritage Dictionary (1985). Second College Edition.
Houghton Mifflin Company. Boston

Azrin, N. H., Bugle, C., & O'Brien, F. (1971). Behavioral engineering:
Two apparatuses for toilet training retarded children. Journal of Applied
Behavior Analysis, 4, 249–253.

Blum, N. J., Taubman, B. & Nemeth, N. (2003) Relationship between
age at initiation of toilet training and duration of training: a
prospective study. *Pediatrics*, **111**, 810–814.

Blum, N. J., Taubman, B. & Nemeth, N. (2004) Why is toilet training
occuring at older ages? A study of factors associated with later training.

Journal of Pediatrics, **145** 107–111.

Brazelton, T. B. (1962) A child-oriented approach to toilet training. *Pediatrics*, **29**, 121–128.

Foxx, R. & Azrin, N.H. (1973). A rapid method of toilet training children. Proceedings of the Annual Convention of the American Psychological Association, pp. 925-926

Free Images (2012). Boy on Pot illustration. Illustrator unknown.

Hagopian, L. P., Fisher, W., Piazza, C. C., & Wierzbicki, J. J. (1993). A water-prompting procedure for the treatment of urinary incontinence. Journal of Applied Behavior Analysis, 26, 473–474.

Horn, I. B., Brenner, R., Rao, M. & Cheng, T. L. (2006) Beliefs about the appropriate age for initiating toilet training: are there racial and socioeconomic differences? *Journal of Pediatrics*, **149**,165–168.

Horstmanshoff, B. E., Regterschot, G. J., Nieuwenhuis, E. E., Benninga, M. A., Verwijs, W. & Waelkens, J. J. (2003) Bladder control in 1–4 year of children in the Eindhoven and Kempen region (The Netherlands) in 1996 and 1966. *Nederland Tijdschrift Voor Geneeskunde*, **147**, 27–31.

Koc,I., Camurdan, A.D, Beyazova,U., Ilhan M.N. & Sahin, F. (2008). Toilet training in Turkey: the factors that affect timing and duration in different sociocultural groups, *Child: care, health and development*, **34**, 4, 475–481.

Luiselli, J. K. (1997). Teaching toilet skills in a public school setting to a child with pervasive developmental disorder. Journal of Behavior Therapy and Experimental Psychiatry, 28, 163–168.

Mahoney, K., Van Wagenen, R. K., & Meyerson, L. (1971). Toilet training of normal and retarded children. Journal of Applied Behavior Analysis, 4, 173–181.

Post, A. Randi & Krikpatrick, Michael A. (2004). Toilet training for a young boy with pervasive developmental disorder. Behavioral

Interventions, 19, 45-50.

Taylor, S., Cipani, E., & Clardy, A. (1994). A stimulus control technique for improving the efficacy of an established toilet training program. Journal of Behavior Therapy and Experimental Psychiatry, 25, 155–160.

8 APPENDIX 1: LIST OF POTTY WORDS

Make	Ca-ca
Number 1	Defecate
Pee	Doody
Pee pee	Dump
Piddle	Feces
Take a leak	Number 2
Tinkle	Poo
Urination/ urinate/ urine	Poopie
Wee	Poop
Wet	Stool
Whiz	

Bathroom, Can, Commode, John, Loo, Potty, Toilet

9 APPENDIX 2: LIST OF POSITIVE PHRASES (COMMENDATION)

These are things you can say to your child, and even to yourself, as you are going through the first two weeks and beyond. When said with a smile on your face and in your eyes, with excitement and enthusiasm, these expressions really help! You should see your child's face "light up" too. Just make sure to vary these, with what you normally say. Like even a good joke, if it is told too many times, it just doesn't work anymore.

Good job!

Hooray!

Yay!

You are a great potty- user!

I knew you could do it!

Wow, look how well you did!

Keep trying!

Keep going!

I can't wait to see you do that again!

Aren't you proud of yourself (with a smile)!

I'm sooo proud of you!

This is fun!

I love spending time with you!

Look at all of that pee/pee (or poopie)!

Wonderful!

You got almost all of it in the potty (with a smile)!

Let's listen for it!

I am so glad you won't have to wear diapers again, aren't you?!

You will be so happy when you can tell everyone, "I am not wearing diapers anymore."!

I love singing the songs with you!

Using the potty makes your body feel better! Hey, "body" and "potty" rhyme!

10 APPENDIX 3: "INGREDIENTS" LIST

These are things that you may want to consider buying/having as you start to potty-train your child:

Paper towels

A bleachable towel

Bleach

Some fun books to read to/with your child

A toothbrush

Potty-training DVD/ videotape/ media

A movie/set of shows that you and your child are interested in watching

A portable potty seat

A step stool (to reach your bathroom sink)

A package of pull-up type, intermediary undergarments

A package of children's underwear

Several pairs of sweatpants, or other comfortable bottoms with an elastic waistband

11 APPENDIX 4: "BATTLE OF WILLS" RESPONSES

This appendix is a bit harder to write, because each individual interaction is different, but here are some things you can try. Often times if it has gotten to the point where you are head to head with your child, one of you is going to lose. You must remember that neither of you wants to be the one to lose, especially if your child is older than 3 years. My husband and I had a wonderful ballroom dance coach (before we had the children), who said that dancing is not about leading and following, but about letting your partner have your way. This advice is very appropriate here as well. It is easier to avoid the battle than to fight it. Therefore instead of asking a yes/no question, ask a "when" question, e.g. "Do you want to use the potty in one minute or 3 minutes?"

Below are some other similar phrases and questions that can get you started with figuring out your own best way to avoid the fight, still get your way, AND allow your child the independence and thought that he/she came up with the decision.

"I'm going to race you. Who will get to the potty first?"

When you know the child has to go, but doesn't want to, you can say the above. Then pretend to get up and race him/her, allowing him/her to win.

"I see the potty dance, but I know you will go to the potty yourself without my telling you."

When you see the child dancing a bit. Here you allow him/her to go to use the potty without direct instruction to do so.

"I am going to use the potty in 3 minutes. When are you going to use it?"

The point is that you leave the child enough time to go first, but not enough time such that if he/she wants you to go first, he/she has an accident.

"Do you want to try to use the potty 5-8 times today or 8-10 times today? It's a lot but I think you can do it!"

By giving the child a choice of how many times he/she wants to try to use the potty, you have leverage all day. In the afternoon, you can say, "You are doing great. You have used the potty 3 times so far. You only need 3 more tries to get what you wanted/ meet your goal. Do you want to try now, so we can add it?"

"I know you said you don't need to try, but let's see if your body will surprise you if you sit on the potty and count to 10 (or say your abc's). Let's see what will happen."

Personal Notes: (Please feel free to use this area to record your own thoughts and ideas)